Piano Quintet in A Major

D667, "Trout"

&

String Quintet in C Major

D956

Franz Schubert

DOVER PUBLICATIONS, INC.
Mineola, New York

CONTENTS

Copyright

Bibliographical Note

This Dover edition, first published in 1999, is a new compilation of two works originally published in Series 4 and 7 of *Franz Schubert's Werke. Kritisch durchgesehene Gesammtausgabe* by Breitkopf & Härtel, Leipzig [1890].

International Standard Book Number: 0-486-40643-1

Manufactured in the United States of America
Dover Publications, Inc., 31 East 2nd Street, Mineola, N.Y. 11501

Piano Quintet in A Major

D667, "Trout"

I

24
30
36
40
pizz.
arco
cresc.
tr

44
tr
p
arco
sf
cresc.
49
54
f
fp
decresc.
59
pp

64
69
73
78
p
fp
cresc.
sf
dim.
tr

82
86
90
94
cresc.
p
pp
tr

98
103
111
116
pp
cresc.
ff
f
p

120
124
128
132
cresc.

137
144
cresc.
149
158

167
171
175
179
p
dim.
f
a 2.
tr

183
187
191
196
cresc.
p
f
cresc.

202
dim.
dim.
dim.
dim.
207
pizz.
213
arco
pizz.
arco
220
pizz.
cresc.

225
arco
pizz.
arco
231
cresc.
237
cresc.
242
decresc.

246
250
254
259
decresc.
cresc.
dim.

264
tr
268
273
tr
278
p
p
p
p
tr

283
287
291
295
p
f
ff

299
cresc.
cresc.
cresc.
cresc.
cresc.
303
8
pp tranquillo
308
8
cresc.
314
cresc.
cresc.
cresc.
cresc.
cresc.

II

21
fp
sf
24
p
27
30
decresc.

33
36
39
43
fp
a 2
8
p
pp
de-

46
cresc.
cresc.
cresc.
cresc.
49
dim.
dim.
dim.
pp
pp
decresc.
ppp
dim.
decresc.
pp dolce
54
57
pp

80
82
84
87

90
decresc.
decresc.
93
pp
pp
96
fp
fp
a 2.
fp
fp
100

104
pp
decresc.
decresc.
decresc.
decresc.
107
dim.
pp
dim.
pp
dim.
pp
dim.
dim.
112
decresc.
decresc.
decresc.
decresc.
decresc.
ppp
ppp
ppp
ppp
pp dolce
117
pp

III
Scherzo.
Presto.
Presto.
11
22
32

41
a 2.
50
60
70

81
94
Trio. 105
116
decresc.

127
pp
pp
pp
dim.
dim.
dim.
dim.
138
f
f
f
f
149
1
p
p
p
p
161
tr
1.
2.
Scherzo da Capo.

IV

30
35
Var. II.
42
46
p
p
p
p arco
mf
1.
2.
tr

50
55
Var. III.
61
64
p
fp
a 2.
f
tr
stacc.

67
1.
2.
p
a 2.
p
1.
2.
69
p
p
8
72
8
75
8

78
Var. IV.
81
ff
fp
85
89
pp
tr

92
tr
decresc.
pp
p
96
cresc.
dim.
Var. V.
101
8
107
1.
2.

113
pp
pp
p
pp
pp
118
pp
decresc.
123
dim.
dim.
dim.
dim.
dim.

128
Allegretto.
p
Allegretto.
3
p
133
p
138

144
149
154
160
p

166
dim.
decresc.
dim.
decresc.
dim.
V
Finale.
Allegro giusto.
Allegro giusto.
11
23

33
pp
pp
a 2
f
f
f
f
f
sf
sf
sf
sf
42
p
p
p
a 2
f
f
f
f
f
54
sf
sf
sf
sf
p
63
fp
fp
fp
fp
fp

72
pp
dim.
ppp
pp
dim.
dim.
84
mf
sf
92
100
decresc.
pp

110
8
pp
122
8
cresc.
decresc.
134
p
dolcissimo
pp
142
8

150
158
166
174

183
191
199
208
dim.

217
229
239
252

263
274
286
297
a 2.

307
pp
dim.
ppp
pp
dim.
320
mf
sf
328
336
decresc.
tr

346
pp
359
cresc.
decresc.
pp
dolcissimo
372

379
8
386
8
f
mf
mf
sf
f
393
f
mf
mf
sf
p
f
p
f
f
f

401
408
416
423

431
442
452
464
p
dim.
ff
f
p
ff

String Quintet in C Major

D956

I

34
40
47
52
cresc.
fp
ff
fz
f
p

57
f
pp
pizz.
fp
decresc.
65
dim.
72
80
arco

87
pp
pp
pp
pp
pp
decresc.
decresc.
decresc.
decresc.
decresc.
94
decresc.
decresc.
decresc.
decresc.
decresc.
fp
fp
fp
fz
100
p
pp
pp
pp
stacc. sempre
p
104
decresc.
decresc.
decresc.
decresc.
decresc.

108
decresc.
decresc.
decresc.
decresc.
112
cresc.
cresc.
cresc.
cresc.
cresc.
116
decresc.
decresc.
decresc.
decresc.
arco
cresc.
cresc.
cresc.
cresc.
cresc.
122
decresc.
decresc.
decresc.
decresc.
decresc.

127
dolce
dolce
tr
132
tr
137
fz pp
fz pp
fz pp
fz pp
fz pp
fz pp
fz pp
fz pp
fz pp
fz pp
146
p
pp
dim.
fz
p
pp
dim.
fz
p
pp
dim.
fz
pp
dim.
fz
p
pp
dim.
fz

155
p cresc.
165
cresc.
173
180
decresc.

188
196
pp
pp
pp
pp
pp
204
f
fz
p
212
decresc.
p

218
226
234
241
p
pp
mf
fz

246
251
256
262
cresc.
ff
fz
ffz
pp
p
f

270
279
cresc.
cresc.
cresc.
288
cresc.
cresc.
298

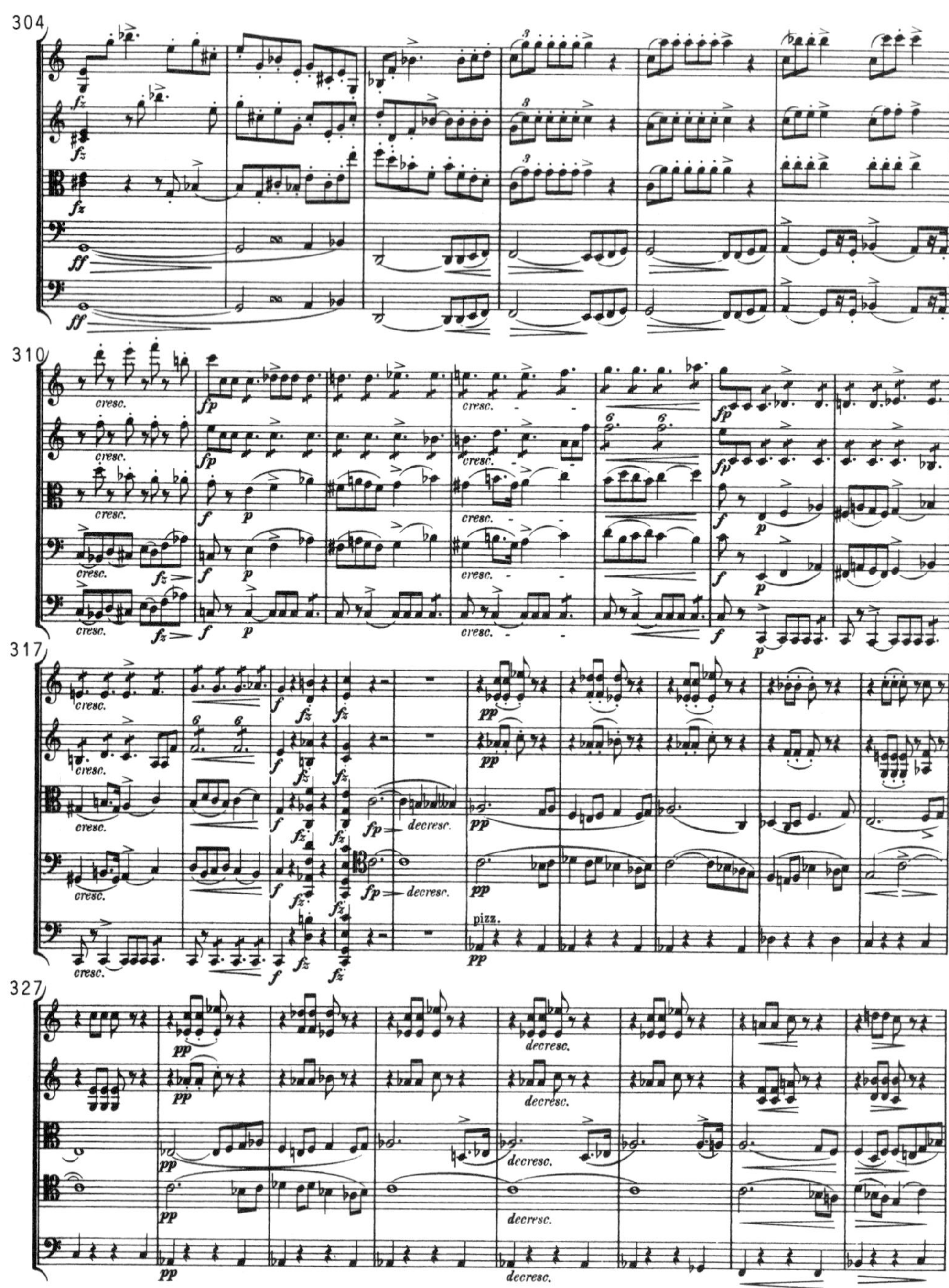
304
310
317
327
fz
ff
cresc.
fp
f
p
decresc.
pp
pizz.

335
pp
decresc.
fp
344
351
358
stacc.
fz
p

364
decresc.
368
decresc.
372
p
cresc.
376
arco
f

381
decresc.
p
cresc.
f
decresc.
387
p
392
397
tr
fz>pp

405
414
423
431
p
pp
dim.
ff
fz
ffz
cresc.
decresc.
tr

II

19
arco
cresc.
pizz.
arco
pizz.
arco
pizz.
arco
f
dim.
p
pp
25
ppp
dim.
cresc.
29
ff
fz
31

33
cresc.
cresc.
cresc.
cresc.
cresc.
35
p
p
p
p
p
cresc.
cresc.
cresc.
cresc.
cresc.
37
f
f
f
f
f
cresc.
cresc.
cresc.
cresc.
cresc.
ff
ff
ff
ff
ff
decresc.
decresc.
decresc.
decresc.
decresc.
39
p
p
p
p
p
p
p
dim.

41
p
pp
pp
p
p
f
f
f
f
f
decresc.
decresc.
decresc.
decresc.
decresc.
43
p
p
p
p
p
dim.
dim.
dim.
dim.
dim.
45
p
p
p
p
p
cresc.
cresc.
cresc.
cresc.
cresc.
47
ffz
ffz
ffz
ffz
ffz
decresc.
decresc.
decresc.
decresc.
decresc.
p
p
p
p
p

49
pp
cresc.
51
ff
ffz
53
decresc.
p
55
dim.
pp

57
dim.
dim.
dim.
dim.
dim.
ppp
ppp
ppp
ppp
ppp
ppp
ppp
ppp
ppp
ppp
61
ppp
ppp
ppp
ppp
ppp
pp
pp
pp
pp
pp
65
67
cresc.
cresc.
cresc.
cresc.
cresc.

69
decresc.
dim.
dim.
decresc.
decresc.
71
pizz.
arco
73
cresc.
cresc.
cresc.
cresc.
cresc.
decresc.
decresc.
decresc.
decresc.
decresc.
75
pizz.
arco

77
pizz.
arco
ppp
dim.
80
cresc.
84
f
decresc.
p
87
pp
ppp

25

37
p
cresc.
fz
47
cresc.
f
57
68
fz

77
86
95
105

118
130
147
158
cresc.
cresc.
cresc.
cresc.

167
176
185
198
cresc.
f
fz
p
ff
fff
tr

Trio.
Andante sostenuto.
215
223
234
243
mf
cresc.
f
p
pp
tr
decresc.

251
tr
cresc.
p
ppp
dim.
260
Tempo I.
p
cresc.
Scherzo D. C.
IV
Allegretto.
fz
9

18
26
35
45
ff
fz
p
f
cresc.

54
p
p
p
p
59
65
p
71
pp
pp
pp
pp
pp

78
p
fz
fp
86
p dolce
92
97

102
108
114
125
mf
fz
p
f
cresc.
pp
tr
decresc.
pp espressivo

135
ppp
ppp
ppp
ppp
ppp
145
155
cresc.
cresc.
cresc.
cresc.
cresc.
165
ff
ff
ff
ff
ff
ff
ff
ff
ff
ff

174
182
190
198

207
216
223
decresc.
230

237
243
251
260
fz
decresc.
pp
ritard.
a tempo
p

271
fz
fz
fz
p
p
278
284
p
289
p

295
301
307
318
cresc.
decresc.
pp espressivo

328
dim.
dim.
dim.
dim.
ppp
ppp
ppp
ppp
ppp
338
349
cresc.
cresc.
cresc.
cresc.
cresc.
360
fff
fff
fff
fff
fff

Più allegro.
370
fz
p
cresc.
377
f
cresc.
ffz
384
fz
ffz
392
fff

400
Più presto.
406
412
420
cresc.